MAY   2017

Eva and Ethan

Kelly Doudna

Consulting Editor, Diane Craig, M.A./Reading Specialist

ABDO
Publishing Company

Published by ABDO Publishing Company, 4940 Viking Drive, Edina, Minnesota 55435.

Printed in the United States.

Credits
Edited by: Pam Price
Curriculum Coordinator: Nancy Tuminelly
Cover and Interior Design and Production: Mighty Media
Child Photography: Steven Wewerka, Wewerka Photography
Photo Credits: AbleStock, Brand X Pictures, Comstock, Corbis Images, Kelly Doudna, Photodisc

Library of Congress Cataloging-in-Publication Data

Doudna, Kelly, 1963-
     Eva and Ethan / Kelly Doudna.
          p. cm. -- (First sounds)
     ISBN 1-59679-146-2 (hardcover)
     ISBN 1-59679-147-0 (paperback)
       1. English language--Vowels--Juvenile literature. I. Title. II. Series.
     PE1157.D683 2005
     428.1'3--dc22
                                                                                  2004059903

SandCastle™ books are created by a professional team of educators, reading specialists, and content developers around five essential components that include phonemic awareness, phonics, vocabulary, text comprehension, and fluency. All books are written, reviewed, and leveled for guided reading, early intervention reading, and Accelerated Reader® programs and designed for use in shared, guided, and independent reading and writing activities to support a balanced approach to literacy instruction.

Let Us Know

After reading the book, SandCastle would like you to tell us your stories about reading. What is your favorite page? Was there something hard that you needed help with? Share the ups and downs of learning to read. We want to hear from you! To get posted on the ABDO Publishing Company Web site, send us e-mail at:

sandcastle@abdopub.com

SandCastle Level: Beginning

Ee

ABCDEFGH
IJKLMNOPQ
RSTUVWXYZ

abcdefgh
ijklmnopq
rstuvwxyz

Eva

Ethan

ears

eagle

east

eraser

easel

Look at my .

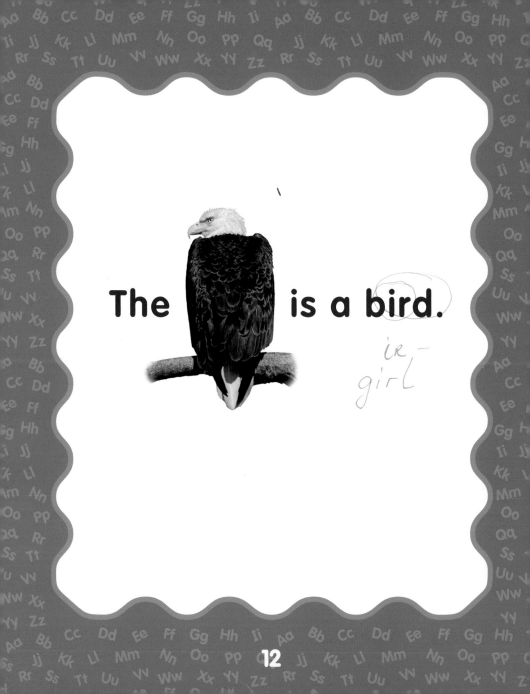

The _____ is a bird.

*ir —
girl*

Look to the .

The is pink.

Here is the .

Eva paints at the easel.

Ethan is in the painting.

Ethan has big ears!

Which of these pictures begin with **e**?

More words that begin with e

easy

eat

eel

e-mail

enough

equal

even

evening

About SandCastle™

A professional team of educators, reading specialists, and content developers created the SandCastle™ series to support young readers as they develop reading skills and strategies and increase their general knowledge. The SandCastle™ series has four levels that correspond to early literacy development in young children. The levels are provided to help teachers and parents select the appropriate books for young readers.

Emerging Readers
(no flags)

Beginning Readers
(1 flag)

Transitional Readers
(2 flags)

Fluent Readers
(3 flags)

These levels are meant only as a guide. All levels are subject to change.

To see a complete list of SandCastle™ books and other nonfiction titles from ABDO Publishing Company, visit **www.abdopub.com** or contact us at:
4940 Viking Drive, Edina, Minnesota 55435 • 1-800-800-1312 • fax: 1-952-831-1632

and Eason